It's My State!

NEBRASKA

The Cornhusker State

Doug Sanders and Pete Schauer

Cavendish
Square

New York

Published in 2017 by Cavendish Square Publishing, LLC
243 5th Avenue, Suite 136, New York, NY 10016

Library of Congress Cataloging-in-Publication Data

Names: Sanders, Doug, 1972- author. | Schauer, Pete, author.
Title: Nebraska / Doug Sanders and Pete Schauer.
Description: New York : Cavendish Square Pub., [2017] | Series: It's my state! | Includes index. | Description based on print version record and CIP data provided by publisher; resource not viewed.
Identifiers: LCCN 2015045113 (print) | LCCN 2015044157 (ebook) | ISBN 9781627132497 (ebook) | ISBN 9781627132473 (library bound)
Subjects: LCSH: Nebraska--Juvenile literature.
Classification: LCC F666.3 (print) | LCC F666.3 .S26 2014 (ebook) | DDC 978.2--dc23
LC record available at http://lccn.loc.gov/2015045113

Editorial Director: David McNamara
Editor: Fletcher Doyle
Copy Editor: Nathan Heidelberger
Art Director: Jeffrey Talbot
Designer: Joseph Macri
Senior Production Manager: Jennifer Ryder-Talbot
Photo Research: J8 Media

NEBRASKA
CONTENTS

★ State Flower: Goldenrod

Several varieties of goldenrod thrive in Nebraska. In the 1800s, Ida Brockman, daughter of a state lawmaker, wrote this of the flower: "It is native, and only a true native should be our representative. It has a long season, and nothing could better represent the hardy endurance of Nebraska's **pioneers**." Goldenrod was declared the state flower in 1895.

★ State Bird: Western Meadowlark

The western meadowlark was adopted as the state bird in 1929. This symbol of the plains is known for the bubbling tones of its gentle song. Well adapted to prairie life, these birds nest on the ground in secluded areas in fields and meadows.

★ State Tree: Cottonwood

When Nebraska was still a territory, cottonwoods served as important landmarks for pioneers heading west. In 1937, the American elm was chosen as the state tree. In 1972, the state legislature selected the cottonwood. A tough tree associated with the pioneer spirit, cottonwoods can be found throughout the state.

NEBRASKA

POPULATION: 1,826,341

★ State Mammal: White-Tailed Deer

In 1981, the state legislature named the white-tailed deer the official state mammal. These plant eaters are a common sight in the forests, meadows, and cornfields of the state. Males have antlers that they shed in the winter and grow again in early spring. Females typically give birth to one or two white-spotted fawns.

★ State Fish: Channel Catfish

This popular sport fish can weigh up to 60 pounds (27.2 kilograms). It gets its cat-related name from the eight "whiskers" growing from its chin. These are actually barbels covered in taste buds. You can identify channel catfish by their narrow heads, forked tails, and rounded fins. The channel catfish was named the state fish in 1997.

★ State Gemstone: Blue Agate

Blue agate, also called blue chalcedony, was declared the state's official gemstone in 1967. It is often found in northwestern Nebraska and can be used to make jewelry. Although it is often blue in color, it has been found in other colors as well.

Wild irises and prairie grass flourish at
Agate Fossil Beds National Monument
in northwestern Nebraska.

The Cornhusker State

The landscape of Nebraska is as varied as its people. Towers of rock jut into the sky, like lookouts stationed above the rolling prairie. Shallow rivers and streams drift across the state. Many are bordered by cliff-like formations called buttes. They have steep sides and flat tops. Gentle, sloping plains mark much of the state. The land gently rises in elevation from east to west.

One word that could be used to describe Nebraska is timeless. Rambling across the state, it's possible to imagine the Native Americans who once hunted the plains or the long trains of prairie schooners, or covered wagons, that slowly rolled their way west. The state's forested bluffs and tallgrass prairies have changed little since these first settlers entered the state.

Still, Nebraska has seen many changes. What military **explorer** Stephen Long called the "Great Desert" in 1820 is now dotted with manmade lakes and reservoirs. Suburbs and cities have come to a land where once the only skyscraper was the spire of Chimney Rock in the western part of the state.

It's the state's balance of close-knit communities and wide-open spaces, of the timeless landscape and the modern world that many Nebraskans find so appealing. From rushing rivers and vast prairies to the wild moonscapes that mark parts of its Panhandle, Nebraska has it all. As one resident of Chadron noted, "It's America's best-kept secret."

The Missouri River, which forms the eastern border of Nebraska, winds its way close to Decatur.

Eastern Nebraska

The Missouri River forms the entire eastern **border** of the state. It runs along part of the state's northern border as well. Nebraska is the only state located entirely within that great river's basin. "Big Muddy," as the Missouri River is often called, is a lifeline to the region, a major waterway known for its rich history and varied beauty. Lined in places by chalkstone bluffs, the river's many islands and sandbars serve as reminders of the challenges early riverboat captains faced as they chugged along the gentle waters.

Gentle valleys and rolling hills mark this part of the state. The crests, or tops, of these often-steep hills are generally rounded, worn down by years of erosion. The hills are partly made up of what is called glacial till. Millions of years ago, massive glaciers had spread into the heart of the North American continent. As the **climate** changed and the last Ice Age ended, these giant sheets of ice slowly retreated north. Along the way, they tilled, or churned and ground up, the soil beneath. What was left behind was a deep and rich layer known as till. Later, dirt and dust carried by the wind (and known as **loess**) added another layer to the Nebraskan landscape. Loess makes up the eastern third of the

Nebraska Borders	
North:	South Dakota
South:	Kansas Colorado
East:	Iowa Missouri
West:	Wyoming Colorado

state, including the region south of the Platte River. Over the years, rivers and streams cut their way through the region. Today, farms and communities mark this part of the state.

The Great Plains

For many, when they think of Nebraska, the first image that comes to mind is the Great Plains. Stretching westward, nearly three-quarters of the state is covered by the prairies and grasslands that make up the Great Plains and mark the American heartland. This plains region stretches beyond the state line into neighboring Wyoming and Colorado.

Included in this area are the High Plains, reaching into north-central and western Nebraska. With its towering rock formations, steep buttes, eroded hills, and deep canyons, this part of Nebraska offers some of the state's most unusual sights. The western stretch of the High Plains contains its own share of rugged beauty. Blanketed in evergreen trees, Wildcat Hills and Pine Ridge offer some of the state's most memorable scenery.

From its southeastern corner to the High Plains of the west, the state slowly gains elevation. Near the border with Wyoming, the land is more than 1 mile (1.6 kilometer) above sea level. It's not surprising that the area is home to the state's highest point. Found in Kimball County in the southwestern tip of the Panhandle, Panorama Point reaches 5,426 feet (1,654 meters) above sea level.

Loess covers the central and southern plains. The landscape here is not as flat as many believe. Rolling hills break up the flatter, wide-open spaces. In south-central Nebraska is

The treeless prairies of Nebraska forced settlers to build homes out of sod.

NEBRASKA
COUNTY MAP

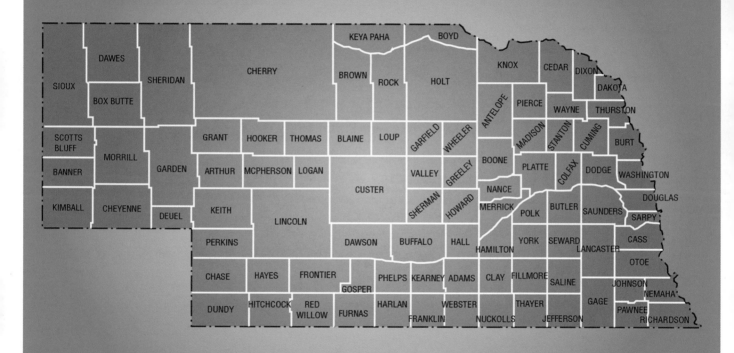

Adams	31,364	Boyd	2,099	Chase	3,966
Antelope	6,685	Brown	3,145	Cherry	5,713
Arthur	460	Buffalo	46,102	Cheyenne	9,998
Banner	690	Burt	6,858	Clay	6,542
Blaine	478	Butler	8,395	Colfax	10,515
Boone	5,505	Cass	25,241	Cuming	9,139
Box Butte	11,308	Cedar	8,852	Custer	10,939

NEBRASKA
POPULATION BY COUNTY

County	Population	County	Population	County	Population
Dakota	21,006	Johnson	5,217	Saline	14,200
Dawes	9,182	Kearney	6,489	Sarpy	158,840
Dawson	24,326	Keith	8,368	Saunders	20,780
Deuel	1,941	Keya Paha	824	Scotts Bluff	36,970
Dixon	6,000	Kimball	3,821	Seward	16,750
Dodge	36,691	Knox	8,701	Sheridan	5,469
Douglas	517,110	Lancaster	285,407	Sherman	3,152
Dundy	2,008	Lincoln	36,288	Sioux	1,311
Fillmore	5,890	Logan	763	Stanton	6,129
Franklin	3,225	Loup	632	Thayer	5,228
Frontier	2,756	Madison	34,876	Thomas	647
Furnas	4,959	McPherson	539	Thurston	6,940
Gage	22,311	Merrick	7,845	Valley	4,260
Garden	2,057	Morrill	5,042	Washington	20,234
Garfield	2,049	Nance	3,735	Wayne	9,595
Gosper	2,044	Nemaha	7,248	Webster	3,812
Grant	614	Nuckolls	4,500	Wheeler	818
Greeley	2,538	Otoe	15,740	York	13,665
Hall	58,607	Pawnee	2,773		
Hamilton	9,124	Perkins	2,970		
Harlan	3,423	Phelps	9,188		
Hayes	967	Pierce	7,266		
Hitchcock	2,908	Platte	32,237		
Holt	10,435	Polk	5,406		
Hooker	736	Red Willow	11,055		
Howard	6,274	Richardson	8,363		
Jefferson	7,547	Rock	1,526		

Source: US Bureau of the Census, 2010

a heavily farmed part of the prairie called the Loess Plains. Flat and regular, it covers roughly 7,000 square miles (18,130 square kilometers).

In general, the plains receive little rain, which often poses a threat to farmers. Nebraska's farmers have led the way in developing systems of **irrigation** that help them make a living out of the land. Nebraskans are the largest producers and users of center-pivot irrigation. This system allows more water to be spread over a larger area with less waste. However, new research is showing that center-pivot irrigation may be damaging to aquifers. An aquifer is a layer of rock or sand that absorbs and holds water.

The Sandhills

North-central Nebraska stands out as the location of a unique geographical feature. The Sandhills are the largest stable sand-dune groupings in the Northern Hemisphere. Still considered a part of the Great Plains, the Nebraska Sandhills were probably blown in from the west, first forming nearly ten thousand years ago. When Zebulon Pike passed through the region, he wrote, "This area may in time become as famous as the deserts of Africa." While his prediction did not come entirely true, it's still a unique region nonetheless.

The Sandhills cover about 20,000 square miles (51,800 sq km), or one-fourth of the state. The surrounding region is dotted with marshes and lakes. This is Nebraska's cattle

The Sandhills, held in place by a grass covering, are the largest stable sand dune grouping in the Northern Hemisphere.

country. The area's wealth of water—in the form of streams and wells—and rich supply of grass have helped ranching to thrive.

The wind has played a major role in shaping this part of the state. It has shifted and piled billions of grains of sand to form the ridges and hills that seem to fold back onto themselves. Some consider Sandhills the wrong name for the region, as there is little sand in sight. Instead, tall and short grasses grow on a thin layer of soil covering the dunes. The grasses filled in and helped to bind the surface of the Sandhills, holding them in place.

Once a rip or crack is opened in this fragile surface, though, the contents underneath begin to spill out. The sand is lifted and carried by the wind, and soon a deep dent is left in the earth. These are called blowouts. They are usually patched by placing layers of old tires or even entire old cars in the holes. This makes the area around the blowout more stable and encourages the grass to return, repairing and resealing the holes.

The Panhandle

The Panhandle is home to some of the state's most striking features. Toadstool Geologic Park marks a part of the state commonly called the Badlands. Here, the land buckles and folds, twisting and turning into a vast array of unusual shapes. The "toadstools," or mushrooms, found in the park are actually slabs of sandstone perched on top of "stems" made of brule clay. These strange formations were sculpted by wind and water over thousands of years. The soft clay bases eroded more quickly than their sandstone caps and

Sandstone mushroom caps sit on clay stems in Toadstool Geologic Park.

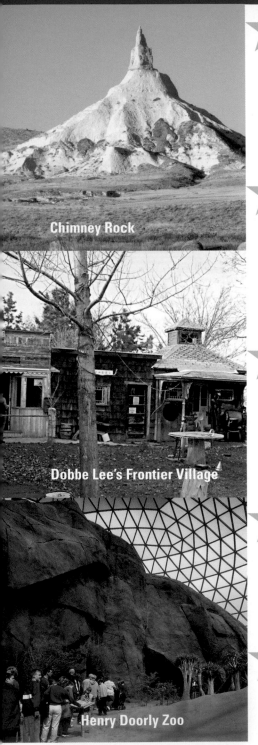

Chimney Rock

Dobbe Lee's Frontier Village

Henry Doorly Zoo

1. Agate Fossil Beds National Monument

There are so many bones from animals that lived here nineteen million to twenty-one million years ago that it is one of the world's most significant mammal sites from the Miocene epoch. Included are bones from the *Menoceras*, a North American rhinoceros.

2. Chimney Rock

Located in western Nebraska, this rock formation impressed first the Native Americans and then pioneers on the Oregon, California, and Mormon Trails. Dubbed "Chimney Rock" in 1827 by Joshua Pilcher, the structure was designated a national historic site in 1956.

3. Dobbe Lee's Frontier Village

Alliance is where Dobbe Lee's Frontier Village, a town with buildings that date back to the 1890s, calls home. It contains buildings from the 1890s through the Prohibition period, with each building within the village containing furnished materials from that time.

4. Henry Doorly Zoo

The Henry Doorly Zoo in Omaha was dubbed the world's best zoo by TripAdvisor in 2014. It features exhibits including an aquarium, the largest indoor desert and largest indoor rainforest, and Stingray Beach, where you can touch and feed stingrays.

5. Rowe Sanctuary

Located in Gibbon, the Iain Nicolson Audubon Center at Rowe Sanctuary is a wildlife preserve known for protecting the lives of sandhill cranes, whooping cranes, and other birds

NEBRASKA

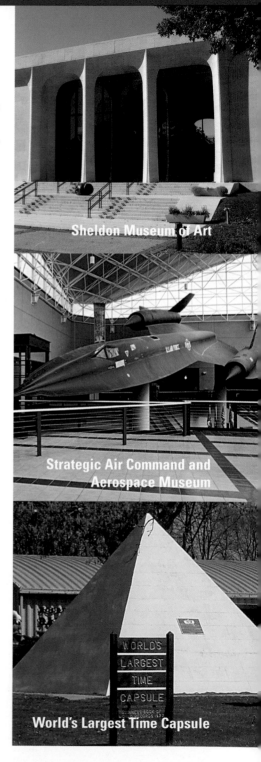

6. Sandhill Journey Scenic Byway

The drive along Highway 2 from Grand Island to Alliance exposes travelers to some of the best sites Nebraska has to offer. Attractions along the route include the Stuhr Museum of the Prairie Pioneer and the Valentine National Wildlife Refuge.

7. Sheldon Museum of Art

The Sheldon Museum of Art was initiated in 1929 and resides on the campus of the University of Nebraska-Lincoln. With more than twelve thousand pieces, the museum boasts one of the world's most comprehensive collections of twentieth century North American art.

Sheldon Museum of Art

8. Strategic Air Command and Aerospace Museum

This museum in Ashland teaches visitors about science while they are having fun. There are motion rides, a planetarium, a space shuttle slide and bouncer, historic warplanes, spacecraft, and plenty of activities.

Strategic Air Command and Aerospace Museum

9. Sunken Gardens

Originally known as the "Rock Garden," the Sunken Gardens in Lincoln are the only Nebraska garden listed in *National Geographic Guide to America's Public Gardens: 300 of the Best Gardens to Visit in the US and Canada*

10. World's Largest Time Capsule

Harold Keith Davisson created the 45-ton (40.8–metric ton) time capsule in Seward, which made the 1977 *Guinness Book of World Records* for the world's largest time capsule, to show his grandchildren what his life was like. He included a leisure suit and a Chevy Vega.

World's Largest Time Capsule

thus suggested the shape of giant mushrooms. Eventually the toadstools collapse under the weight of the sandstone. However, new ones continue to form to replace them.

Climate

In a state where farming is so important, climate and weather can be major concerns. A period with little or no rain, called a **drought**, can be devastating. While southeastern Nebraska can receive up to 30 inches (76.2 centimeters) of rain and other precipitation each year, the Panhandle is much drier, with averages totaling 17 inches (43 cm) per year. In recent years, droughts affecting the state have ranged from mild to severe. There is little that can be done to control the weather, though. To show how important the subject is, the state has set up two agencies to focus on weather issues and concerns. The Climate Assessment and Response Committee and the Nebraska State Climate Office study weather trends and provide forecasts and advice in dealing with the often-harsh conditions.

Nebraska has a mild climate. Warm summers, cold but not-too-snowy winters, lots of sunshine, and average humidity are the rule. Nonetheless, state residents have learned to adjust to the occasional seasonal extremes. Nebraskans also know that the expected can turn into the unexpected in a flash. Early evening thunderstorms are common events in the summertime, especially in the eastern and central portions of the state. The sky blackens and thick masses of clouds churn in the sky. Nebraska is located squarely in the line of what is called America's Tornado Alley. Nebraskans know that at certain times, when storms arrive, it's best to run for cover. Many tornados have ripped across the state, causing terrible damage and threatening lives.

Nebraska experiences extreme weather because of its location in Tornado Alley.

Storm chasers, people who follow and study tornados and other dramatic weather events, find Nebraska a prime hunting ground for violent weather. A team of these curious thrill seekers travels throughout the Midwest in the spring and summer. They drive special storm-chasing vehicles, equipped with Doppler radar and other devices that allow them to collect data and to track and study storms. Another storm-chasing tool is the tornado-intercept vehicle. These armored vehicles are equipped with IMAX cameras and allow film crews to drive inside the swirling and dangerous storm systems.

Name Change

The state's nickname was originally the "Tree Planter's State," but in 1945 it was changed to the "Cornhusker State."

Wildlife

Although forests cover only 2 percent of the state, Nebraska still has its share of trees. Oaks, elms, box elders, basswood, ash, and hackberry are just a few of the trees that can be seen wafting in the prairie winds. One of the state's major wooded areas can be found along the Niobrara River valley. It took root in the moist, rich soil and spread from the east, almost halfway across the state. To the northwest, the rugged Pine Ridge region is another trove of tree life. As its name implies, it's an area known for its impressive stands of pine.

The habitat of the once common prairie chicken has been greatly reduced.

Perhaps the state's most impressive forest, though, is the product of its hardworking residents. The first US Forest Service nursery in the country is the Nebraska National Forest. Located near Halsey, it's the country's largest woodland planted entirely by hand. The forest was originally created to draw potential settlers to the otherwise barren region. Few settlers came, but the trees helped curb erosion and prevent the dusty topsoil from being carried away by the wind.

The most common form of plant life in the Cornhusker State is the wealth of native prairie grasses for which the state is known. These varied species house, hide, and feed an equally impressive array of animal life. Mule deer, white-tailed deer, pronghorn antelope, bison, elk, and bighorn sheep are just a few of the four-footed creatures that make the state their home. Coyotes and bobcats pad across the prairie in search of food, while along the state's rivers and streams, beavers, muskrats, and minks thrive. Raccoons are drawn to the water as well, to try their hand at fishing. Trout, perch, bass, catfish, carp, pike, and crappies abound beneath the surface of the state's many waterways.

Nebraska is a bird watcher's paradise, with many people descending on the state each year to view migrating sandhill cranes. Dedicated birders also enjoy the mating calls and elaborate dances of the sharp-tailed grouse. Pheasants, quails, ducks, snow geese, turkey vultures, whippoorwills, great horned owls, and wild turkeys are among the species found in the state. Golden eagles and prairie falcons soar over the grasslands, their sharp eyes searching for rodents and prairie dogs below. Cliff swallows also make an annual appearance in Nebraska. They fly more than 3,000 miles (4,828 km) from Argentina to nest in the state's lake-filled southwestern corner.

Endangered

With so many natural treasures, Nebraskans have made strong efforts to protect the land and the life it supports. The state has fifteen species of plants and animals on its list of endangered species. Programs and agencies have been created to make sure the list does not grow. Black-footed ferrets, for example, once roamed the plains freely. With

Late Night Snack

The Reuben sandwich was allegedly created in Omaha in the 1920s at the request of Lithuanian immigrant Reuben Kulakovsky. He ordered it made during his regular late-night poker game at the Blackstone Hotel.

the arrival of settlers from the east, their population, along with those of several other animals, went down. Today, there have been reports of black-footed ferrets in the wild, but there are no known populations in the state.

Sometimes the best **conservation** plans help to protect animals long before a species is threatened or endangered. Every year, more and more visitors flock to the 80-mile (129 km) stretch of the Platte River to witness the annual migration of more than five hundred thousand cranes. The birds have become a popular attraction each March, as they stop along the river to rest and feed before flying on to their breeding grounds in Canada, Alaska, and parts of Siberia. About 80 percent of the world's population of sandhill cranes passes through the region every year.

The increased **tourism** has helped the economy of this part of the state. Still, many local residents, biologists, and officials have realized that this economic success must not come at a cost to the birds. While the birds have been traveling to the area for thousands of years, if their habitat is harmed or threatened, or if they feel pressured, they may choose another stopping location on their annual migration.

Migrating sandhill cranes gather in the Platte River near Kearney.

Black-Tailed Jackrabbit

Black-Tailed Prairie Dog

Coyote

1. Black-Tailed Jackrabbit

Found in Nebraska, the black-tailed jackrabbit can run at a top speed of 30 miles per hour (48 kilometers per hour) and can jump 20 feet (6 m) in distance, which is especially helpful when running away from predators like coyotes, bobcats, foxes, badgers, and weasels.

2. Black-Tailed Prairie Dog

The black-tailed prairie dog can grow to between 12 and 16 inches (30 and 40 cm) and can weigh up to 2.5 pounds (1.1 kilograms). The species' population has been steadily increasing in recent years. The average lifespan is three to four years

3. Cottonwood

Cottonwoods can be found throughout the state. They can grow to 66 to 145 feet (20 to 45 m) in height. These trees are grown for timber production and provide food for many butterfly and moth species.

4. Coyote

The coyote is a relative of the wolf. These highly intelligent animals are mostly active at night, when their sharp barks and howling can be heard drifting across the plains. Coyotes eat birds, insects, dead animals, rodents, and rabbits.

5. Goldenrod

Goldenrod, which was declared Nebraska's state flower in 1895, can be found in multiple areas within the state, dry or wet, including woods, prairies, and shores. Goldenrod is often yellow, and is sometimes a cream or white color.

6. Little Bluestem

Also known as bunch grass or beard grass, little bluestem is found across the Great Plains. It commonly grows in clumps of up to three hundred reddish purple stems, which turn a golden color as the plant ages.

7. Prairie Chicken

This peculiar bird, a member of the grouse family, was once an important food source for Native Americans and settlers living on the plains. Through the years, the range and number of the prairie chicken have greatly decreased. It is known for its foot-stomping mating dance.

8. Prairie Rattlesnake

The prairie rattler is one of only four species of poisonous snakes living in Nebraska. Mostly active in the daytime, these reptiles live off a diet of rabbits, prairie dogs, kangaroo rats, mice, and lizards.

9. Pronghorn Antelope

Most of Nebraska's pronghorns are found in the western Panhandle, but smaller populations are located in the Sandhills and central areas of the state as well. Drought and the spread of farms have affected the antelope population.

10. Sandhill Crane

Sandhill cranes have been stopping over in Nebraska during their annual migrations for thousands of years. More than half a million birds gather each spring along the Platte River before heading to their summer breeding grounds.

Prairie Rattlesnake

Pronghorn Antelope

Sandhill Crane

Dinosaurs once dominated the landscape of what is now Nebraska, and they left behind fossils in Agate Fossil Beds National Monument as proof.

From the Beginning

Humans first entered the central plains around twelve thousand years ago, near the end of the last Ice Age. They were mostly hunters, following roving herds of big game. These people, often called the Paleo-Indians, were the ancestors of the Native Americans who would eventually spread across the state and take over. "Paleo" means older or ancient. Over thousands of years, these ancient peoples lived on the grasslands that would become the future state of Nebraska. Slowly, weather and climate patterns shifted and became more stable, allowing for more people to settle on the land. This, as well as the extinction of several prehistoric species such as the mammoth, encouraged the creation of more permanent settlements. The Paleo-Indians continued hunting and gathering, but eventually they started to farm plots of land in and near their villages.

By two thousand years ago, more complex communities dotted the plains. These early residents made helpful, everyday items out of pottery. They also fished in Nebraska's many rivers and grew to rely more heavily on **agriculture** for survival. Nebraska was a harsh region to conquer. Periods of drought forced some groups to pack up and search for a better life elsewhere. During times of prosperity, many sought out the future state. The region quickly became a crossroads of Native American life. Even in its earliest days, the state had a lively and diverse mixture of Native languages and culture groups.

This image of Big Elk was painted in 1832 by famed frontier artist George Catlin. Big Elk was an Omaha warrior.

Native Nebraska

The region that was to become Nebraska was settled by several mighty Native American nations. They came to dominate the central plains well into the 1830s. The Pawnee and their northern relatives, the Arikaras, left perhaps the deepest mark on the region. They first arrived in Nebraska from the south and were well established there by the mid-1500s. They built earthen lodges made of stacked poles covered with brush and packed with mud. These striking structures were a common sight, grouped into villages huddled along the banks of the Platte, Loup, and Republican Rivers, to name a few. Pawnee men were hunters and sometimes went to war for their people, while the women were responsible for farming, cooking, and child care. While only men became tribal chiefs, the women also took part in the storytelling activities as well as art and music.

Other groups left their mark as well. The Cheyenne, Arapaho, and Lakota (Teton Sioux) pushed west after originally settling in the forests north and east of the Missouri River. The Omaha, Ponca, and Otoe were also transplants to the area. They entered the eastern portion of the state in the 1700s and lived in the Missouri River basin as well. By the start of the 1800s, about forty thousand Native Americans called Nebraska home.

The arrival of European explorers and settlers changed the Native Americans' lives forever. The introduction by the Spanish of the horse meant they could travel and hunt more effectively. New diseases such as measles and smallpox swept through entire villages, leaving very few standing. Eventually the valuable land the Native Americans held was too tempting to arriving settlers, and the Native people were slowly driven from the land. Treaties were made. However, not all the land deals between the US government and the various Native nations had been made final by the 1850s, when the area became a territory that was suddenly opened for settlement. The Homestead Act of 1862 saw many Natives forced off of their land and into **reservations**, which are now managed by the US Bureau of Indian Affairs.

The First Europeans

The first European to make an appearance in the region was a Spaniard, Francisco Vázquez de Coronado. He and a crew of men trekked across the American Southwest in 1541, making it all the way to Kansas. The explorer claimed the entire region for Spain, and to this day, Coronado's expedition is known for making the first European sightings of both the Colorado River and the Grand Canyon.

Coming from a different direction, French explorer René-Robert Cavelier, sieur de La Salle, sailed down the Mississippi River in 1682. Though he did not set foot in the future state, he claimed all the land drained by the river for King Louis XIV, the ruler of

The first explorers in the region traveled on foot and by canoe as they mapped the land and its rivers.

The Native People

This photo from 1871 shows a Pawnee family outside its earthen lodge near Loup.

Long before settlers arrived in Nebraska, the state was home to various Native tribes, including the Omaha, Pawnee, Otoe, Santee Sioux, Winnebago, Ponca, Iowa, and Sac and Fox. The Pawnee tribe largely dominated the Native American population, with an estimated four thousand to five thousand people living in the state. When the Nebraska Territory was set up in 1854, an estimated ten thousand Native Americans were living in the eastern portion of what is now the state, where they set up permanent villages along the Missouri and Platte Rivers.

While there were a lot of differences among the various tribes living in Nebraska at the time, there were also some similarities. For example, most of the tribes spoke branches of the Siouan language family, though the Pawnee spoke a Caddoan language and the Sac and Fox spoke an Algonquian language. Many of the Native tribes farmed and hunted the numerous bison.

When tribes such as the Delaware were pushed into Nebraska in the 1800s, they fought the original residents for valuable land. In 1854, the US Congress created the Kansas and Nebraska territories under the Kansas-Nebraska Act. As a result of that act, the 1860s saw the American government force many of the Native American tribes out of the Nebraskan lands and onto reservations. Despite being located in the United States, reservations are legal designations of land that are managed by the US Bureau of Indian Affairs. With the government forcing Native Americans off of their land and into what was called Indian Territory in what is now Oklahoma, Americans and Europeans migrated to Nebraska and settled there under the Homestead Act.

Six of the eight original tribes are now federally recognized tribes living on their own reservations in Nebraska: the Iowa, Omaha, Ponca, Sac and Fox, Santee Sioux, and Winnebago. The Iowa and Sac and Fox tribes are actually part of two states, with Kansas being the other.

Spotlight on the Omaha

Omaha is pronounced "oh-muh-hah" and means "upriver people." The tribe is governed by councilmembers who are elected by the tribal members.

Distribution: The Omaha tribe currently occupies the Omaha Reservation, 12,421 acres (5,027 ha), located in Thurston County, with sections also located in Cuming and Burt Counties.

Food: The Omaha were big-game hunters, following buffalo herds during the spring and summer. While their diet consisted mostly of meat, the Omaha tribe would harvest corn, beans, and squash during the fall. In the winter, they ate dried food, fish that they caught in the river, and small game that was hunted.

Clothing: Omaha men wore breechcloths with leather leggings and buckskin shirts, while the women wore long dresses made of deerskin. Both the men and women wore moccasins on their feet. Omaha people later adapted to European clothing like cloth dresses and vests, which were decorated with beads. Women usually wore two long braids in their hair, while male warriors would sport a Mohawk or shaved head with a scalp lock, which was one long bunch of hair on top of their heads. Both men and women wore tribal tattoos and would paint their faces for special occasions.

Art: The Omaha tribe is famous for various forms of art, including quilling, beading, and hide paintings.

Transportation: For longer trips that involved carrying belongings, the Omaha used drag sleds, called travois, pulled by dogs and later horses.

France. This was just the first step in opening the region to curious Europeans seeking their fortune along the American **frontier**. During the 1690s and early 1700s, trappers and traders crisscrossed the region. By 1714, the French explorer Étienne Veniard de Bourgmont had followed the course of the Missouri River all the way to the mouth of the Platte River.

With competing claims on the continent, Spain and France became rivals for power and control of the New World. The Nebraska region became one source of the conflict. Feeling the French had overstepped their bounds, Spaniard Pedro de Villasur led a group of forty-five men into the area in 1720 with the hopes of expelling, or removing, the French. Before they could do so, though, Pawnee warriors near the Platte River attacked the group while they were sleeping.

Napoléon Bonaparte sold France's land west of the Mississippi to the United States in 1803.

In the battle that followed, thirty-six of the Spaniards were killed, including Villasur himself. While this ended the Spanish impact on the central Great Plains, the French remained in the region, holding tightly to their foothold in Nebraska.

In 1739, French explorers Paul and Pierre Mallet, joined by six others, left Illinois in the hope of reaching present-day Santa Fe, New Mexico. Along the way, they crossed almost the entire length of Nebraska. They also named the Platte River. Slowly the territory that was to become Nebraska was being mapped and tamed. Events in Europe would cause the region to change hands several times. In 1763, after a costly war in Europe, France gave up all of its land claims west of the Mississippi River to Spain. Like before, though, French fur traders were still working in the now Spanish-controlled region.

For the time being, they were wise in staying. In 1800, French leader Napoléon Bonaparte forced the Spanish to return the land. French control was to be short-lived, though. Three years later, in need of funds, Bonaparte sold the large territory, in a deal referred to as the Louisiana Purchase, to the US government.

The Americans Arrive

With so much newly acquired land, the Americans and President Thomas Jefferson were eager to explore their recent purchase. Meriwether Lewis and William Clark and their Corps of Discovery spent three months in the state, starting in 1804. They traveled up the Missouri River and explored what are now the eastern and northern borders of Nebraska. Then, in 1806, US army captain Zebulon Pike, on a similar mission, entered and explored south-central Nebraska as part of the Pike Expedition.

It was not long before trading posts sprang up in the Missouri River valley. The Spanish-American trader Manuel Lisa established a string of them from 1807 to 1820. Fort Lisa, one of the posts, was located 10 miles (16 km) from present-day Omaha. Lisa worked to form alliances with local tribes, like the Omaha, and was even appointed US Indian agent by the governor of the Missouri Territory. Lisa also married the daughter of Big Elk, who was the principal chief of the Omaha tribe until 1846, and the marriage was seen as a strategic alliance. The economy of this once-remote region was developing

This log home is located on the grounds of Fort Atkinson State Historical Park. The fort was the first military post built in Nebraska.

Making a Native American Headdress

What You Need

About twenty colored craft feathers, depending on the size of the headdress

Strong paper such as oaktag, poster board, or corrugated bulletin board border, to make your headband

Measuring tape

Liquid glue

Colored pieces of paper cut into squares about the same height as the headband

Colored pieces of paper cut into circles about 1 inch (2.5 cm) in diameter

Tape

What To Do

- Ask someone to measure the distance around your head, passing the tape around the forehead. Record the measurement and add about 2 inches (5 cm). Cut a piece of strong paper to the length that you measured. It should be 3 to 4 inches (7.5 to 10 cm) tall.

- Glue the colored squares to the front of the headband. You can turn some so they are diamonds. Glue the circles in the middle of the squares and diamonds. Do this until the front of the headband is decorated.

- Once the glue dries, turn over the headband (this is now the back) and glue down the feathers.

- Once that glue dries, check to see if the point of any feather is sharp. Put a piece of tape over any sharp points to prevent poking or scratching.

- Place the headdress around your head, and have someone secure it in place by taping the ends together. Have them use the two extra inches for an overlap. The headdress should cover your forehead, and not rest on top of your hair.

slowly. Trappers and traders, looking to cash in on the wealth of furs they could find to the west, continued to pass through the region. In 1812, fur agent Robert Stuart left Astoria in the Oregon Territory and headed for New York City. Entering Nebraska in 1813, Stuart and his seven companions followed the course of the North Platte River to the point

where it joins the South Platte. They continued, following the river until it met up with the Missouri River. It proved to be an ideal path to follow and would later become the course of the Oregon Trail, which brought countless pioneers deep into the American West.

In 1819, the US Army arrived to build Nebraska's first military post, Fort Atkinson. It was established near the present-day town of Fort Calhoun, located in Washington County. Intended to protect the American frontier, the site became, along with the village of Bellevue, one of the largest communities in Nebraska. With more than one thousand residents, Fort Atkinson set up the state's first school, library, and gristmill. The fort was eventually abandoned in 1827.

A year after the army arrived, Major Stephen Long—who was recognized for his design of steam locomotives—and a group of twenty men followed the South Platte to its source near present-day Denver, Colorado. Major Long's now-famous reports talk of a barren and harsh land, unfit for humans. He held little hope that the region would one day prosper. On the simple map that a member of Long's expedition drew, the major had this area, which includes present-day Nebraska, labeled the "Great Desert." Long felt that this area of land would be better served as a buffer against other nations who shared the continent with the United States, including the Spanish, British, and Russians. Long's expedition also provided accurate descriptions of Omaha, Otoe, and Pawnee life and customs.

Luckily, Major Long's impressions were wrong. Nebraska would become a thriving territory in no time. Missionaries appeared, including the famed Catholic priest Father Pierre-Jean de Smet, who was eager to work with the Nebraska and Pawnee Native Americans. Fur traders continued to come and go, spreading through the region. They especially flocked to the Platte River route, which quickly grew in popularity. In little more than two decades, Long's great desert awould become flooded with thousands of pioneers, eager for a better life in the American West.

The Territory Grows

As more and more American settlers searched for their fortunes in the West, Nebraska became an important center of activity. Both the Oregon Trail and the Mormon Trail wound their way through the region. Pony Express riders followed the well-worn routes that traveled through the Platte River valley. Before the arrival of the railroad, steamboats were important to the trade and transportation of the region.

With so much increased traffic, Fort Kearny was built to offer added protection for the hopeful pioneers headed west. Though white settlers flooded the area, most were only passing through.

By the 1840s, Nebraska was on the road to statehood. Secretary of War William

These cottonwoods are still standing on the site of Fort Kearny, but the buildings were taken down.

Wilkins, in a report from 1844, stated, "The Platte or Nebraska River being the central stream would very properly furnish a name to the territory." It was in that year that the first attempt was made to make the area a territory. The measure failed to pass, however. Another bill, known as the Kansas-Nebraska Act, was eventually approved in 1854 after much debate and disagreement. The act overturned the Missouri Compromise of 1820. That law drew a line across the United States and its territories, allowing **slavery** south of the line but prohibiting slavery north of the line. The Kansas-Nebraska Act officially created the Kansas and Nebraska territories—both were north of the line—and provided new land for settlement, while also allowing the citizens of the new territories to decide whether or not slavery would be allowed. Voting to allow or prohibit slavery was called popular sovereignty. There was violence in Kansas as people supporting both sides of the issue rushed into the territory to try to tilt the vote in their favor.

The two new regions were created in the hope of increasing settlement west of the Missouri River. Originally, the Nebraska Territory was much larger than the state is today. In addition to Nebraska, it included parts of the present-day states of Montana, Wyoming,

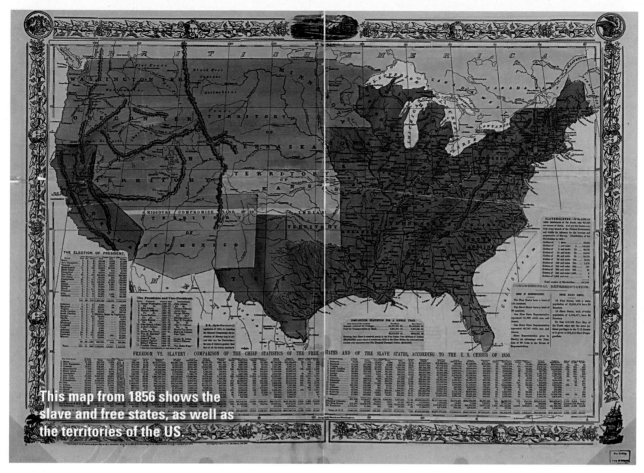

This map from 1856 shows the slave and free states, as well as the territories of the US.

Colorado, and North and South Dakota. By 1863, the territory had been divided further, leaving Nebraska close to the size and shape it is today.

By the 1850s, the nation was deeply divided over the issue of slavery. Those opposed to the practice were worried that the new territories would allow slavery. Those in favor of slavery believed there was no question that it should be allowed in the newly created lands. The two sides clashed, and minor conflicts were fought in the region long before the first cannons of the Civil War were fired. (The slavery issue was the main reason for the Civil War.) Slaves were first bought and sold in Nebraska in the 1850s in Nebraska City. Most Nebraskans were against the practice, and in 1861, the legislature of the territory passed an act to abolish slavery.

Slavery was not the only issue dividing the newly created territory. Residents and officials disagreed over how the territory would be settled, the creation of new laws, the coming of the railroad, and, most notably, the location of the territorial capital. In addition, there were often regional rivalries between those living north of the Platte River and those who had settled to the south. Many issues remained to be worked out, and the territory was denied statehood when it first attempted to join the Union. Still, the area

Omaha

Lincoln

1. Omaha: population 408,958

Founded in 1854, Nebraska's largest city is home to five *Fortune* 1,000 companies as well as the Henry Doorly Zoo. During June, Omaha is flooded with baseball fans, as the College World Series is played in Ameritrade Park each year.

2. Lincoln: population 258,379

The capital of Nebraska, Lincoln is home to the University of Nebraska as well as the second-tallest capitol building (398 feet or 121 m) in America. It was founded in 1856 as "Lancaster" before being renamed Lincoln.

3. Bellevue: population 50,137

Bellevue, which is French for "beautiful view," was incorporated in 1855 and is known as the oldest continuously functioning town in the state of Nebraska. Bellevue is the site of Offutt Air Force Base.

4. Grand Island: population 48,520

Grand Island hosts the Nebraska Law Enforcement Training Center (NLETC), which trains all officers throughout the state. The area was settled in 1857, when German settlers found what was then known as "La Grande Isle" in the Platte River.

5. Kearney: population 30,787

The city of Kearney was originally called Dobytown and was actually located two miles southeast of the current location. The city was moved and renamed after Fort Kearny. It is known as the Sandhill Crane Capital of the World.

6. Fremont: population 26,397

Named after American explorer and military official John C. Frémont, the city was planned in 1856 with the hope that the railroad would extend to the city. Fremont hosts many different industries and is home to Hormel, the maker of SPAM.

7. Hastings: population 24,907

Hastings is most famous for being the location where Kool-Aid was created, by Edwin Perkins in 1927. The drink is still celebrated there to this day, with the Kool-Aid Days festival every August.

8. North Platte: population 24,733

The North Platte Canteen, a railroad stop where citizens provided refreshments and supplies for soldiers, was located here during World War II. The city is also the site of the Buffalo Bill Ranch State Historical Park.

9. Norfolk: population 24,210

The city was founded by forty-four German Lutheran families who arrived in July 1866. The 321-mile (517 km) Cowboy Trail, the longest rail-to-trail conversion in the United States, runs from Norfolk to Chadron.

10. Columbus: population 22,111

This small city in Platte County was home to Andrew Jackson Higgins, who designed and produced Higgins boats, the landing craft used by US soldiers during invasions in World War II. It was also a post for outfitting pioneers in the nineteenth century.

North Platte

Columbus

prospered. From 1854 to 1860, Nebraska's population grew from 2,732 to 28,841.

The Civil War and Beyond

During the Civil War, which began in 1861, the residents of the Nebraska Territory generally supported the Union, or Northern, forces. Volunteers helped form the First Nebraska Infantry under the command of Colonel John M. Thayer.

Civil War battles never entered the territory and affected the region less than they did the states located farther to the east.

The passage of the Homestead Act in 1862, which was signed by President Abraham Lincoln, increased the territory's population all the more. It granted settlers who were twenty-one years of age or older, or the head of the family, 160 acres (65 hectares) of free western land if they agreed to live and work on it. More hopeful pioneers came to try their hand at working the Nebraska countryside. The Homestead Act would go on to grant 1.6 million homesteads of federal land, or 10 percent of all land in the United States from 1862 to 1934. The major event of the 1860s was the coming of the Union Pacific Railroad. A line extending westward from Omaha was started in 1865. It reached the western

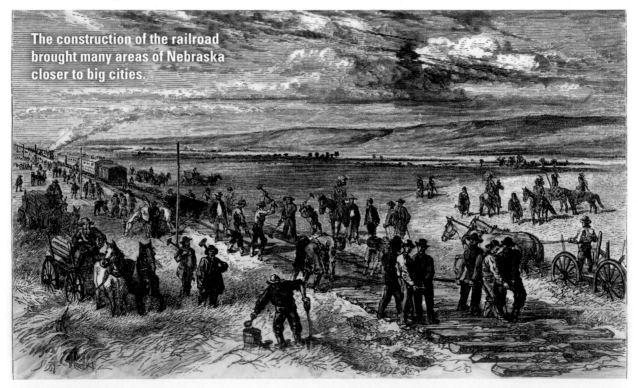

The construction of the railroad brought many areas of Nebraska closer to big cities.

This resourceful family used thick blocks of sod to build a home in Custer County in the 1880s.

border of the territory two years later. Throughout the 1870s and 1880s, the railroads were big business in the state and did much to change life in the region. To spur the growth and number of railroad lines and to further connect the growing country, the US government offered certain companies portions of the territory in the form of land grants.

To raise funds in order to build the rail lines, the companies in turn sold large tracts of the land to interested settlers. They often created elaborate ad campaigns to lure new arrivals, not only from the East Coast but from Europe as well. The ad campaigns worked. Along with a flood of former Civil War soldiers who also arrived in the region in search of land, the population of Nebraska ballooned to almost 123,000 by 1870. By the mid-1880s, the Burlington Railroad lines also crossed the state. Once-remote areas now found themselves in greater contact with the world beyond.

Statehood

Nebraska was finally admitted to the Union on March 1, 1867, but again, not without conflict. The president serving at the time, Andrew Johnson, was a Democrat and did not want the mostly Republican territory to be offered statehood. He vetoed, or rejected, the act of Congress making Nebraska a state. Congress was able to override Johnson's veto. However, lawmakers set down their own terms the territory had to meet before it was allowed into the Union. The Nebraska legislature had to remove a phrase from its proposed state constitution that gave only free white men the right to vote.

The early years of statehood were rough on Nebraska. It was a pattern that had become all too familiar. As was the case for some of Nebraska's early Native cultures, the harsh conditions of life on the prairie proved too challenging for some residents. When swarms of grasshoppers descended on the state and destroyed **crops**, many farm families packed up and headed back east. The state's economy did not surge in the 1870s, and recovery was slow in coming.

By the 1880s, though, the tide had turned. Another large wave of settlers came to the state. New residents, eager for their own homesteads, arrived on the plains. Land prices increased steadily throughout the decade. Once again, however, with the arrival of the 1890s, the state faced hard times. Drought settled on the land, and real estate prices dropped. Many farmers found themselves bankrupt.

Settlers, such as this family that moved to the Loup Valley in 1886, had to overcome many hardships.

People called out for change. Farmers felt banks and railroads were concerned only with their own profits. Families and other small operations could not afford the high prices the railroads charged to ship crops and other farm products. Hundreds of Nebraska farmers turned to a new organization called the Farmers' Alliance. It worked to reduce shipping costs and curb the power of large companies.

The most famous person who spoke out against the large companies was William Jennings Bryan. He was raised in Illinois, but he moved to Nebraska in 1887 and was elected to congress three times, starting in 1890. He thought government should protect people and the government from businesses that were monopolies. A monopoly controls trade or a service. Bryan was so persuasive in his speeches that he was nominated as the Democratic Party's candidate for president three times. However, he lost all three elections.

The Twentieth Century

Nebraskans had long been inventive when it came to coaxing a living out of the often-harsh landscape. New techniques had been developed for irrigating, or watering, the dry soil. To help the state along, Congress passed the Reclamation Act in 1902. It created funds to encourage and improve irrigation systems in twenty states in the western portion of the United States, such as the North Platte Project, which helped irrigate 165,000 acres (66,773 ha) of Nebraskan land. In the Panhandle, where farming could be especially challenging, new crops were able to thrive. Sugar beets, alfalfa, and winter wheat are major crops still grown in the state today.

In central and western Nebraska, farmers and ranchers had often clashed. Ranchers often resented the presence of farmers, who claimed land the ranchers felt could be better used for raising cattle. With Congress's passage of the Kinkaid Act, though, the farmers scored a victory. The Kinkaid Act, which was signed by President Theodore Roosevelt in April 1904, allowed farmers to increase their holdings up to 640 acres (259 ha) at no cost and thus have a greater chance to make a success of their ventures. The act served thirty-seven counties in northwest Nebraska, where the Sandhills were located. As a result of the act, the Sandhills saw greater development. Though many found the area too harsh to farm successfully, their efforts still helped build the area's economy. While the Sandhills did not lend themselves easily to farming, it was ideal cattle country. Ranchers bought the failed farms and fattened their herds on the grassland.

Drought caused the land to dry out and erode during the Great Depression.

In 1917, World War I brought great change to the nation, especially Nebraska. While many brave Cornhuskers were off fighting in Europe, the state's economy boomed. There was a great demand for the wealth of farm products Nebraska produced. With the end of the war in 1918, though, the economy slumped once again. Then came the ultimate blow in 1929. The Great Depression gripped the country and eventually the world. Jobs were scarce, people were out of work, and there was little relief in sight. The price of farm products dipped even further. Yet another drought only made matters worse. Farmers lost their land. Relief in the form of long-term, low-interest loans provided some help, but the lean years left few Nebraskans untouched.

Nebraskans were not without hope, though. The coming of World War II in 1941 brought a much-needed boost to the state's economy. Because of the war, farm products were again in high demand, including cattle, oats, wheat, potatoes, and corn. The state's growing number of factories turned out war supplies, and Nebraska was again in an uptick. More than 128,000 Nebraskans joined the war effort, many of them fighting on the battlefields of Europe and Asia.

Improved machinery made it possible for farms to expand greatly after World War II.

In the last half of the twentieth century, the state's economy changed rapidly. Agriculture began to change, with the state's farms becoming larger but fewer in number. The size of the average farm almost doubled between 1950 and the late 1990s. Meanwhile, the number of farms was reduced by half. Advances and new developments in technology and farm machinery signaled a change in times, as it meant that larger operations would now require fewer workers. Many Nebraskans needed to look for new ways of earning a living. Some turned to the state's cities and towns as important sources of income. During the 1960s, state leaders were able to attract new businesses, mostly in manufacturing, to the state.

As the state's economy and centers of population shifted, new challenges arose. Once a mostly rural state, Nebraskans were faced, more and more, with problems often associated with larger cities, such as crime, urban poverty, and racial unrest due to the mixed feelings

Room for Everyone

The world's largest porch swing, located in Roosevelt Park in Hebron, can seat twenty-four children or sixteen adults.

of the past regarding slavery. The 1960s were a period of radical change for Nebraska's African-American residents. **Civil rights** demonstrations, which were held to call attention to racial inequality, took place in Omaha in 1963. Then, in 1968 and 1969, race riots in that city, coupled with a fifty-four-student sit-in at the University of Nebraska at Omaha, required the US military and the National Guard to step in.

Meanwhile, in rural Nebraska, farmers faced challenges of their own. Farming became too expensive for some because there was little profit to show for the hours of labor required. Many families sold their farms and turned to another way of life. By 1970, more than 60 percent of the state's residents lived in Nebraska's cities and towns. The times marked a major shift away from rural life. The change made Nebraskans aware of the need to build industries and to draw new business to the state. In the twenty-first century, many residents look to the future with confidence. They also continue to honor their roots and the times of struggle and triumph that have made the state the strong, united place it is today.

10 KEY DATES IN STATE HISTORY

1. March 1714

Étienne Veniard de Bourgmont becomes the first recorded European to enter the area now known as Nebraska.

2. May 29, 1739

While trying to find the way to Santa Fe, Frenchmen Pierre and Paul Mallet become lost and are the first Europeans known to cross Nebraska.

3. April 30, 1803

With the Louisiana Purchase, in which the US acquired 828,000 square miles (2.1 million sq km) of land from France, the United States gains possession of what is now Nebraska.

4. May 30, 1854

Congress passes the Kansas-Nebraska Act, allowing the new territories to decide whether or not slavery will be allowed within their borders.

5. May 20, 1862

The Homestead Act, signed by President Abraham Lincoln, further opens the territory to settlement. Settlers twenty-one years of age and older are able to get 160 acres (65 ha) of land for free.

6. March 1, 1867

Nebraska joins the Union as the thirty-seventh state, and the capital is moved from Omaha to Lincoln.

7. April 28, 1904

The Kinkaid Act, introduced by Moses Kinkaid and signed into law by President Theodore Roosevelt, serves as an amendment to the Homestead Act. It promotes settlement in the Sandhills and the Panhandle.

8. October 29, 1929

The stock market crashes and the Great Depression begins.

9. December 13, 2006

Federal Circuit Court of Appeals upholds a district court ruling that Nebraska's Initiative 300 is unconstitutional. The state law, passed in 1982, barred farmers from selling their land to corporations.

10. November 6, 2015

President Barack Obama rejects a request from TransCanada to build the Keystone XL pipeline, a proposed oil line. Residents opposed its route through Nebraska over environmental concerns.

This farm family reflects the ethnicity of the early white settlers of Nebraska, which is becoming increasingly diverse.

The People

Nebraskans have always been a diverse group. The state's first residents were the Native Americans who settled comfortably in the open grasslands in more than fifteen tribes. Even to this day, the Native Americans embody what Nebraska is all about, which is history and culture, and they are still a large part of the population that makes up the state. Other newcomers arrived as slaves, while still more came from Europe in search of a better life. Today, Nebraskans trace their roots to a variety of sources. Many know that home is where the heart is, coming from families who have lived in the state for many generations.

More than four-fifths of Nebraska's population lives in the eastern part of the state. Omaha, the state's largest city, is found there, as well as Nebraska City, Sioux City, and Columbus. With its blend of big-city life and laid-back small-town atmosphere, many find it an ideal setting. Others prefer Lincoln, the state's capital, located less than an hour to the southwest of Omaha. This university town draws students from across the country and around the world.

Through the years, people of varying backgrounds have called the state home. Starting in the 1800s, waves of immigrants began spreading across the plains, especially following the Homestead Act, which was signed in 1862 and led to the Native Americans having to evacuate their land. The largest ethnic groups represented in the state today trace their roots back to Germany, Ireland, England, Sweden, and the Czech and Slovak Republics. But these groups are just one part of the changing face of Nebraska in the twenty-first century. Today, people from across the United States and around the world are drawn to life in the Cornhusker State. From a variety of museums and art spectacles to the world's largest time capsule, there are plenty of reasons to come to Nebraska. Together, Nebraskans form a varied and vibrant society.

Native Nebraska

Nebraska was once home to a long list of Native American groups. The Arapaho, Cheyenne, Dakota Sioux, Santee Sioux, Omaha, Otoe, Pawnee, Potawatomi, Ponca, and Sac and Fox are some of the major groups that made their home on the state's grasslands. These various nations once had more than forty thousand combined members. Through the years, though, their numbers declined. By the early 1910s, less than five thousand Native Americans remained in the state. Most had been forced to move onto reservations in nearby states, especially Oklahoma, due to the overwhelming population of Europeans and Americans taking over their land. The Native Americans signed five different treaties with the US government to cede their land leading up to the signing of the Homestead Act, and all in all, a total of eighteen treaties were signed between the two parties between 1825 and 1892.

A powwow allows Native Americans to celebrate their history and culture.

Today, more than twenty thousand Native Americans call Nebraska home. They are spread across the state in cities and towns and also live on reservations throughout the state. The Iowa, Omaha, Ponca, Sac and Fox, Santee Sioux, and

Winnebago tribes all have federally recognized tribes within the state. A small group of Sac and Fox can also be found living in homes in the southeastern portion of the state.

Each year, usually in July, the Winnebago Reservation hosts a two-day homecoming gathering. Councils are held, and ancient traditions revived and shared. The Santee Sioux and the Omaha also come together and hold celebrations each summer. The events feature a variety of activities. Symbolic dances and traditional songs are performed, bringing the Native past vividly to life. There is also storytelling, during which Native history and lore are shared and passed on. Most of all, these celebrations are a time for Nebraska's Native residents to come together, visit with friends and relatives, and celebrate the bond they share.

Czechs on the Plains

Czechs played a major role in the settling of the Cornhusker State. By 1910, 14 percent of Nebraska's foreign-born residents had come from Czechoslovakia, the largest Czech population in any US state. Crop failures and a weak economy first drove many Czechs from their homeland in the 1870s and 1880s. Many would face similar problems in their new nation. Railroad advertisements—as well as glowing articles in Czech magazines and newspapers—convinced thousands to uproot their lives and try their fortune in the paradise of the American plains. Friends and relatives were a strong draw as well. Their letters and reports home spoke of the pleasures of life on the plains.

Dancers wearing traditional Czech clothing perform in Wilbur.

The newly arrived Czechs were mostly farmers, but merchants and laborers came, too. Many early settlements were almost entirely populated by Czechs. Most immigrants chose to settle together, preferring the comfort and support of their fellow countrymen to ease the transition to life in America. From the mid-1850s until World War I, Nebraska was

★ 10 KEY PEOPLE ★ ★ ★

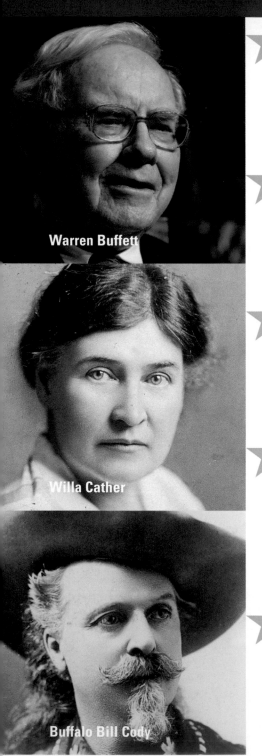

Warren Buffett

Willa Cather

Buffalo Bill Cody

1. Fred Astaire

Known for his acting, singing, and dancing, Fred Astaire called Omaha home in 1899, when he was born. Named the fifth-greatest male star of old Hollywood by the American Film Institute, Astaire won three Emmys and three Golden Globes.

2. Marlon Brando

Although Marlon Brando made his career in New York and called Chicago his hometown, the film star was born in Omaha in 1924. Throughout his career, Brando played major roles in huge movies, including *The Godfather* and *On the Waterfront.*

3. Warren Buffett

Warren Buffett was born in Omaha in 1930 and has been called the "Oracle of Omaha" for his skill in business and investing. He's one of the richest people in the world, with a net worth in late 2015 of about $65 billion.

4. Willa Cather

As a little girl, Cather and her family relocated to a barren stretch of the Nebraska plains. Despite experiencing a difficult and lonely childhood, she grew to love living near Red Cloud. This would fuel her talents as a Pulitzer Prize–winning writer.

5. Buffalo Bill Cody

This colorful character arrived in Nebraska Territory as an eight-year-old boy. By fourteen, he was a rider for the Pony Express. A talented hunter, Cody earned his nickname hunting buffalo on the plains.

6. Alex Gordon

The left fielder on the 2015 World Series champion Kansas City Royals, Alex Gordon was born and raised in Lincoln and was a standout baseball player at Lincoln Southeast High School as well as the University of Nebraska.

7. Malcolm X

In 1925, Malcolm Little was born in Omaha. Malcolm X was a controversial black nationalist and leader in the Nation of Islam. He shed light on racial abuses and called for blacks to throw off racism. Malcolm X was assassinated in New York City in 1965.

8. Red Cloud

Also known as Makhpiya-Luta, Red Cloud was born near North Platte. In 1866 he directed a successful war against the US government, and he dedicated the rest of his life to resisting the advance of settlers.

9. Nicholas Sparks

Novelist Nicholas Sparks has captured the hearts of many young female readers with his writing. Sparks is most famous for writing *The Notebook*, a piece of romantic fiction, in 1996. It was adapted into a movie in 2004.

10. Gabrielle Union

Known for her appearances in movies and television shows such as *Bring It On*, *City of Angels*, *Bad Boys II*, and *Think Like a Man*, actress and model Gabrielle Union was born in Omaha in 1972. Union married NBA star Dwyane Wade in 2014.

Malcolm X

Red Cloud

Gabrielle Union

Who Nebraskans Are

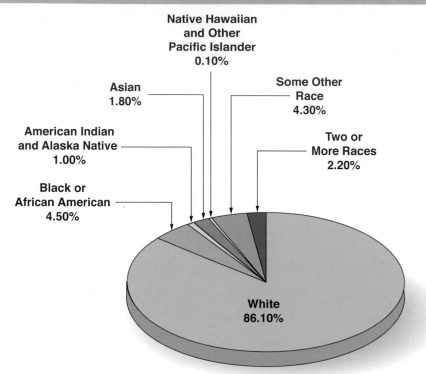

Native Hawaiian and Other Pacific Islander
0.10%

Asian
1.80%

American Indian and Alaska Native
1.00%

Black or African American
4.50%

Some Other Race
4.30%

Two or More Races
2.20%

White
86.10%

**Total Population
1,826,341**

Hispanic or Latino (of any race):
• 167,405 people (9.2%)

Note: The pie chart shows the racial breakdown of the state's population based on the categories used by the US Bureau of the Census. The Census Bureau reports information for Hispanics or Latinos separately, since they may be of any race. Percentages in the pie chart may not add to 100 because of rounding.

Source: US Bureau of the Census, 2010 Census

the top destination for Czechs coming to the United States. As was the case with many plains states at the end of the 1800s, the 1870 census revealed that nearly 25 percent of Nebraskans were foreign born.

Today, many Nebraskans celebrate their Czech heritage in a variety of ways. Festivals and annual events bring the culture to life. Wilber, sometimes called the "Czech Capital of America," draws people from the across the Midwest and beyond to its annual Czech Days festival in the summer. Guests stay in the historic Hotel Wilber and enjoy activities that include a parade, music, dancing, a quilt show, and a talent contest, among many other events. Recently, greater efforts have been made to honor and preserve the history of Czech life on the plains. The Czech Heritage Project is leading the way. Working with groups at the University of Nebraska, project workers are creating an archive, or collection, of photographs and letters that capture elements of early Czech-American life. The collection is available on the Internet for researchers and the public to view. A major part of the project involves translating cassette recordings made in the 1970s by state residents. Mostly told in the Czech language, these oral histories, as they are called, tell of life on the American plains. They are a key part of preserving Nebraska's rich Czech history. Some tell stories of coming to the United States and settling into mostly Czech communities, where children often learned in the Czech language.

Celebrating Trees

Arbor Day was started in Nebraska City by Sterling Morton in 1872 to encourage the planting of new trees and the protection of wildlife.

To keep close ties between the United States and the Czech Republic, the University of Nebraska-Lincoln has set up the Paul Robitschek Czech Study Program. It offers nine-month scholarships to students living in the Czech Republic. Through the program, they are given the chance to further their studies in the United States for two semesters and learn about the place many Czech people immigrated to in the 1800s and 1900s.

African Americans

African Americans have long been a part of the history of the Cornhusker State. The first census of the territory, taken in 1854, listed only four slaves. Up until the Civil War, fewer than one hundred African Americans called the state home. When the war ended—and slavery along with it—this trend changed. Slowly, African Americans began turning to the west as a place to pursue their newfound freedom.

Groups of black settlers soon began pushing into the heart of the plains. Called Exodusters, some came to Nebraska after settling in Kansas for a while. They eventually set down roots in Lincoln, Omaha, and Nebraska City. While many worked for the

The Moses Speese family settled near Westerville in the late 1800s. Many black towns formed in the state at that time.

railroads, others lived mostly in Custer, Dawson, and Harlan Counties. An all-black community was founded at Overton in 1885. More black towns, including Brownlee and DeWitty, formed in the early 1900s in Cherry County. With its large amounts of unclaimed land, western Nebraska became a draw for many black families.

The early decades of the 1900s also marked the great migration to the North. More than 500,000 blacks left their homes in the South and headed north and west. Omaha saw the greatest change. Between 1910 and 1920, its black population doubled from around 5,000 to 10,315. Its population has grown ever since. For many African Americans living in the state, life was not always easy. Racial tensions, killings, and riots marred the lives of many.

Through it all, the state's African-American community has stayed strong. Black Nebraskans still honor the struggles of the past, as they look to the future. Today in Nebraska's schools, the state's African-American heritage is celebrated. As countless students now learn, the history of their state cannot be told without the inclusion of the African-American experience.

New Faces

As is the case in most other states, Hispanics are Nebraska's fastest-growing group. Their numbers nearly doubled during the 1990s. The state's urban areas saw the greatest jump. Douglas County, in particular, which contains the city of Omaha, was the site of the largest rise.

Asian Americans have also grown in numbers. Though a smaller presence in Nebraska overall, the state's Asian community has experienced a major population jump. During the 1990s, it grew by nearly 73 percent.

Hispanics are among the fastest-growing ethnic groups in Nebraska.

Between 2000 and 2010, it grew by another ten thousand people. These figures show the broad appeal of the Cornhusker State.

People from all backgrounds are drawn to the state's peaceful communities, low crime, and strong schools. Nebraska is also an affordable place to live and raise a family. Slowly, Nebraskans are seeing their communities grow and change. While the state is still mostly white, today Nebraska sports its own vibrant blend of peoples and cultures.

The Rural Life

Images of the plains and hearty pioneers making houses out of sod in rural areas are a key part of the state's history. In recent years, however, the state has witnessed a major shift. More and more Nebraskans have moved to urban and suburban centers to build their lives. As farms became larger and required fewer workers, small rural towns struggled to offer other well-paying jobs.

Slowly, communities became drained of their populations. People left in search of better-paying jobs elsewhere. It is a trend occurring across most of the Great Plains. The region has lost more than two-thirds of its rural population since the 1920s. Once-thriving communities are now practically boarded up, just one step away from becoming ghost towns.

Many Nebraskans are trying to find ways to prevent this from happening. One example is the town of Superior in southern Nebraska. The people of Superior know the hardship of losing factories and businesses and the important jobs they provide, so they have joined together, creating an economic development corporation. The goals of the corporation include attracting new businesses to the town and improving existing buildings. Some are hopeful these efforts will lead to a new life for the community.

For now, most residents know that the times have changed and that their towns must change with them. There are no easy solutions. In the meantime, like the people of many of the state's other rural towns, they are trying to come up with ways of coaxing tourists and new businesses to spend and invest money in their town. Still, for many of the people who stay in Nebraska's shrinking towns, the hard times have done little to lessen their love of the rural life. To them, this is the Nebraska they have always known and will always cherish, and it's where they'll continue to raise their families and settle.

John C. Fremont Days

Kool-Aid Days

1. Buffalo Commons Storytelling Festival

Top storytellers and musicians from across the state and the country gather each year in McCook. Cowboy poetry and ghost stories are just part of the fun at this event held around Memorial Day

2. Cottonwood Market Days

This outdoor event, called the Cottonwood Festival until 2013, is held in Hastings in the fall. It features the work of painters, sculptors, glassblowers, and jewelry makers, as well as musical performances, food, and a classic car show.

3. Germanfest

This summer event, held in Syracuse, celebrates the German heritage of many Nebraska residents. A dog race, called the "Viener Race," is held along with "Viener Vogue," a dog fashion show. There are also parades, crafts, food, and a golf tournament.

4. John C. Fremont Days

The people of Fremont gather together in July to celebrate the man who gave their town its name. Dancing, car shows, a reenactment of a frontier camp, and a talent show help to make this tribute complete.

5. Kool-Aid Days

Located in Hastings, the Kool-Aid Days event draws in more than twenty thousand visitors every August to celebrate Edwin Perkins's soft drink invention. Events include a parade, games, entertainment, and the world's largest Kool-Aid stand.

6. Meadowlark Music Festival

Held in Lincoln, this festival celebrates classical music with a series of family-friendly performances. The festival is a great way for people from all backgrounds to experience classical music.

7. Nebraskaland Days

The people of North Platte welcome folks from all around the region to their annual June festival featuring beauty contests, sports tournaments, parades, concerts, rodeos, arts and crafts, and all the food one can eat.

8. Omaha Summer Arts Festival

The Omaha Summer Arts Festival is a free, three-day event in Omaha that features art and music from more than 130 artists throughout the United States in fourteen media, including paintings, sculptures, photography, jewelry and more.

9. Oregon Trail Days

Each July, the town of Gering hosts this top frontier festival, the longest continuously running festival in Nebraska. Visitors enjoy cook-offs, square dancing, an art show, and one of the state's largest parades.

10. Wayne Chicken Show

This fun event is held each July in Wayne. It features a parade, a hot wing eating contest, and plenty of chicken-themed arts and crafts. A "Cutest Chicklette" contest is held for children age four and under.

Nebraskaland Days

Wayne Chicken Show

The rotunda of the Nebraska capitol is magnificently decorated.

How the Government Works

When it comes to their politics, Nebraskans are unique. They are the only people served by a state legislature that is unicameral and nonpartisan. That means the legislature that makes state laws is made up of a single chamber, or house, and that their elections take place without referencing political parties. Most states have two-part legislatures, made up of a senate and a house of representatives, and conduct their elections with Republican and Democratic political parties. For sixty-eight years, Nebraska followed this pattern as well. That was up until 1934, when US senator George W. Norris proposed a change. Following a trip to Australia in 1931, Norris saw the importance of a unicameral system. He felt that it was pointless and a waste of money to have two groups doing the same thing. The idea of switching to a unicameral system was first suggested in 1915, but at that time it was struck down. Some felt it was not a good idea, but it was still debated and discussed in Nebraska for almost two decades. Norris helped to finally end the years of indecision. He proposed an amendment, or change, to the state constitution calling for the creation of the unicameral system.

Those in favor of the plan believed it would make the lawmaking process simpler and more open to the public. They also argued that having a one-house system would save time and money. The new system would also change the way senators were elected. Candidates would not run as part of any official political party—such as Democrat or Republican. They would be judged as individuals and not as members of a larger political group. Voters would decide based on merit, on the strength of a candidates' ideas, and on their records of service.

The voters were given the final say. In November 1934, they voted to adopt the change. The new unicameral legislature first met three years later, in 1937. Norris's predictions turned out to be right. In the unicameral legislature's first year, legislative costs were chopped in half. The state's lawmakers and citizens were convinced they had made the right decision. The change shows the state was not afraid to take a bold step to fit its own unique needs.

George W. Norris proposed that Nebraska adopt a unicameral legislature.

All Kinds of Leaders

State officials are handed the tough task of running Nebraska. They create budgets and then decide how the state will spend its money on a variety of projects and programs. They also create the laws all Nebraskans must follow. These laws decide how fast you can drive on the state's roads and highways, how many days children go to school, and many other issues important to the daily lives of Nebraska's citizens. In a state with so many people, Nebraska's officials try to address the needs and concerns of all.

Representatives in Washington

Nebraska elects two people to serve in the US Senate, as do people in all states, and three people to serve in the US House of Representatives.

Branches of Government

Executive

The governor is the head of the executive branch. He or she prepares the state budget and signs the laws that will best serve the state. A variety of other officials assist the governor. These include the lieutenant governor, secretary of state, attorney general, state treasurer, and auditor of public accounts. Each of these important positions, including the governor, is decided in a general election and carries a four-year term.

Legislative

Nebraska is the only state with a unicameral system of government. That means the state legislature is made up of a single governing body, not two like the US federal government and the other forty-nine states. The Nebraska Unicameral Legislature, often just called "the Unicameral," is made up of forty-nine voting members, called senators, who do not identify or associate themselves with any specific political party. They each serve terms of four years, and can serve no more than two terms in a row. After a second straight term, they must sit out one election before running again.

The capitol is the tallest building in Lincoln.

Judicial

The supreme court is the state's highest judicial body. The governor chooses the chief justice, while the six other judges are selected from each of six districts in the state and serve six-year terms. The state is also served by lesser courts, including courts of appeals, twelve district courts, and courts that hear cases in each of the state's counties.

Work at Home

Most Nebraskans do not need to serve in the capital in Lincoln in order to make a difference. There is plenty to be done in their own counties and communities. Nebraska's cities and towns are grouped to form ninety-three counties. Two-thirds of these counties are run by a board of commissioners. Each board is typically made up of three to five members. Other counties are led by a seven-member board of supervisors. Board members oversee almost all aspects of county business. A variety of people help the board members in carrying out their duties. Clerks, treasurers, lawyers, police officers, and school superintendents are just some of the people who work hard to improve life in Nebraska's counties.

At a more local level, voters choose mayors or boards of commissioners to oversee the daily affairs in Nebraska's many cities, towns, and communities. These public servants play many different roles. They serve as lawmakers and managers. With more than five hundred cities, towns, and villages, it takes a lot of people to make life in Nebraska run smoothly. They make sure the state's citizens have access to government-run services and programs. They also approve the funds for such important tasks as building and improving roads and buying new books for public libraries.

The state funds part of the cost for police and fire protection.

From Bill to Law

A bill is an idea for a new law. It can also suggest ways of changing laws that already exist. A sponsor, usually a state senator, first introduces bills. Sometimes the ideas for laws come straight from ordinary citizens.

Once the senator has presented the bill, it is given a number by the clerk. The title of the bill is then read to the members of the legislature, after which it is sent to the reference committee. This is a group of nine senators who together form the executive board. They will move the bill along to what is known as a standing committee, a group of senators who will look more closely into the issues surrounding the bill. At the same time, the bill is published. Copies are made available to all senators as well as to the general public.

When the standing committee meets to discuss the bill, it holds a public hearing. This important step means the state senators hear from citizens. It gives Nebraskans a chance to express their opinions on issues that are important to them.

If the standing committee approves of the bill, it then goes to what is known as the general file. This is a daily list of bills the senators will be discussing and voting on. They consider all parts of the bill, including any amendments, or changes, the standing committee has made. Then it comes time to vote. If at least twenty-five state senators are in favor of the bill, it is reviewed to be sure it is in its proper form.

More changes can come at any time, which the legislature, again, must approve. The bill is then in its final form. Copies are once again sent to the senators. After the senators have read the entire bill, they take the final vote. If the bill is approved, it is sent to the governor. The governor can sign the bill and make it an official part of state law. He or she can also veto, or reject, the bill. If this happens, three-fifths, or at least thirty members, of the state legislature must still be in favor of the measure for it to become law. Once approved, the bill goes into effect in three months' time. It is then an official part of Nebraska state law.

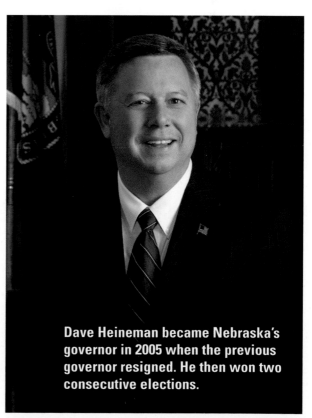

Dave Heineman became Nebraska's governor in 2005 when the previous governor resigned. He then won two consecutive elections.

POLITICAL FIGURES
FROM NEBRASKA

1. John James "Jim" Exon: Governor, 1971-1979; US Senator, 1979-1997

Jim Exon was born in South Dakota and attended the University of Nebraska at Lincoln. After a career in business in Lincoln, he turned to politics and never lost an election. He is one of two Nebraskans (along with George Norris) to win five straight statewide elections. He had wide support for controlling spending and refusing to raise taxes in Nebraska and in the US.

2. Charles "Chuck" Hagel: US Senator, 1997-2009

A decorated Vietnam War veteran from North Platte, Chuck Hagel served two terms as a US senator. A Republican, he served as secretary of defense from 2013 to 2015 under President Barack Obama. He was a critic of the war in Iraq.

3. Kay A. Orr: Governor, 1987-1991

Born in Iowa, Kay A. Orr moved to Nebraska in 1963. She was appointed as state treasurer in mid-term in 1981 and became the first woman elected to a statewide constitutional office when she won an election to return to that post in 1982. She was the first Republican woman elected as governor in US history in 1986, and served one term.

NEBRASKA
YOU CAN MAKE A DIFFERENCE

Contacting Lawmakers

If you are interested in contacting Nebraska's state legislators, go to:

nebraskalegislature.gov/senators

You can search for legislators and their contact information by name, zip code, or district.

To see who represents you in the US Congress, visit this website:

www.govtrack.us/congress/members/NE

Below the photo of each representative is a link to the map of the district they serve.

Give the Cyclists Some Room

In 2012, lawmakers helped to make the cycling community safer when out on the road. Lawmakers, in conjunction with cyclists, helped create a law that Nebraska motorists must leave at least three feet when passing cyclists on the road. The law also covers pedestrians and individuals riding electric scooters. Not obeying the law can result in a citation costing $100 to $300. This type of citation is enforceable if an officer witnesses the infraction, or if there's a car or bicycle accident.

This has helped to make the roads a little safer for cyclists, but there have still been accidents, and even fatalities, at the hands of motorists. That's why Brent Davis, an avid Nebraskan cyclist who had a friend on a bike pass away after being hit by a drunk driver, teamed up with State Senator Rick Kolowski to improve bicycle safety laws in Nebraska. The proposal, also known as Legislative Bill 39, would make it so that motorists would have to follow the same rules when they're passing cyclists as when passing a car, which means that they'd have to change lanes when passing a person on a bicycle. The law would also require cyclists to use a bike path if there's one adjacent to the roadway. The bill had not been passed by the legislature as of November 2015, but the hopes are that it will make the roads a safer place for bicycle riders.

Cattle thrive in the grasslands of Nebraska, which leads the country in the production of red meat.

Making a Living

Nebraska's greatest resources are its rich soil and plentiful water. Hardworking farmers have built Nebraska into one of the nation's leading farming states. The state's success has always been built on its crops and cattle. Through the twentieth century, the state's farms have changed, though. Fewer people now make a living directly from the land. The state's citizens have often been forced to change the way they make a living. New industries have emerged in the Cornhusker State. They offer Nebraskans different choices in the careers they pursue. While large combines and grain elevators are still a common sight in the state, so are businesses and factories that produce and sell a wide range of products.

Agriculture

From meat to beans to grains, many Nebraska products end up on America's dinner tables every day. Farming is not always an easy venture in the Cornhusker State, though. To encourage strong harvests, farmers have adopted a variety of methods that save soil and water. They have led the way in the use of irrigation, crop rotation, and dry farming. Dry farming is a method used in very dry places. Crops that are resistant to drought are planted so there is no need for irrigation.

Good irrigation systems keep millions of acres of Nebraska farmland productive.

The state's major crops include corn, soybeans, dry beans, wheat, hay, grain sorghum, potatoes, and sugar beets. Grapes, tomatoes, and orchard fruits are also grown. The southwestern plateau is wheat country. Sugar beets and dry edible beans are other top crops grown there as well as in parts of the Panhandle. The state leads the nation in the production of great northern beans and produces about 11 percent of all dry beans grown in the United States. In parts of the state where the soil is loose and sandy, many farmers have had success planting potatoes.

Cattle are raised in all of Nebraska's ninety-three counties. The Sandhills, in particular, are prime cattle country. Herds of Angus and Hereford cattle spend the spring and summer feasting on the abundant grasses. Nebraska currently leads the nation in the production of red meat. Though less valuable to the state's economy, hogs, dairy cattle, sheep, and chickens are raised as well. These operations are mostly found in the eastern part of the state, which supports a more diverse economy.

Mineral Wealth

Nebraska is not known for its mining industry. Still, plenty of **mineral** wealth lies locked beneath its soils. Oil and natural gas are found in the Panhandle, mostly in Kimball and Cheyenne Counties. Oil was discovered in the state in 1939. By the early 1940s, several

Delivering Groceries

ConAgra Foods, one of the largest makers of packaged foods in the United States, is based in Omaha.

A worker in Omaha inspects a model of an oil refinery. Oil is extracted from the ground in Nebraska.

companies had begun drilling, and in no time, oil had become the state's most valuable mineral resource.

Sand and gravel are major state products as well. Large quantities are gathered from across the state, but mostly along the Republican and Platte River valleys. Once collected, they are used mostly in concrete and for the surfaces of roads. Similarly, stone is plentiful in the state, mostly in the southern and eastern regions. Limestone, sandstone, chalkrock, and smaller amounts of quartzite are also used in road building and in the creation of cement. Limestone quarries are found along the Missouri River in the state's southeastern stretch. Clay, needed mostly in making tiles and bricks, is another treasure offered up from the Nebraska countryside. It is found across the state and is a major part of the soil of the Badlands.

Tourism

Toadstool Geologic Park, with its wealth of fossils, offers a window into what life was like in the heart of the continent between thirty-eight million and twenty-four million years ago. The park is in a remote area, but the amazing geology rewards visitors. Also, there are campsites available that allow for more exploration. Still visible on some of the rocks are the preserved tracks of ancient animals that passed through the region.

Hugging the southern part of the Panhandle are two impressive landmarks. Chimney Rock stands like a beacon above the plains and can be seen from great distances. It stretches 475 feet (145 m) above the Platte River and is made of brule clay, volcanic ash, and Arickaree sandstone.

Corn

Dry Edible Beans

1. Agricultural Manufacturing

It's only natural that the agricultural manufacturing field is a booming one in the state of Nebraska. Meat processing, specifically beef and pork, are prominent in Nebraska; it's the largest industry in the state when looking at total payroll dollars.

2. Cattle and Calves

Nebraska has more than 23 million acres (9.3 million ha) of range and pastureland, about half of which is in the Sandhills. This vast amount of land has helped the state become the leading producer of red meat in the country.

3. Corn

Corn is the most widely grown crop in the state, with about 10 million acres (4 million ha) used for its production. Corn is used to feed livestock and poultry and produce ethanol, which can be used as a fuel. Corn can even be made into a type of plastic.

4. Dry Edible Beans

Nebraska is the country's third-largest producer of these tiny legumes. Kidney beans, great northern beans, and pinto beans help to keep the nation—and the world—well fed.

5. Finance and Insurance

Nebraska is home to two large financial firms, Berkshire Hathaway and Mutual of Omaha, and is also the birthplace of First Data, a financial transaction processing company that used to be part of American Express.

6. Health Care

Health care is prominent in Nebraska due to the University of Nebraska Medical Center being a major research facility. The University of Nebraska Medical Center has made progress in the public health and aging sectors of the industry.

7. Machinery and Transportation Equipment

Farmers and ranchers need a lot of equipment—tractors, grain elevators, and combines, just to name a few. Nebraska's workers also produce equipment for tractor trailers, trucks, and other giants of the road.

8. Military and Defense Contractors

Since the days of World War II, Offutt Air Force Base has been a major hub for the military and defense industry, hosting more than sixty-five defense contractors and contributing $627 million per year to the Nebraskan economy in company payroll.

9. Sorghum

Sorghum is one of the state's main grain crops. It's used mostly as feed for cattle, hogs, and chickens. It is well suited to the Nebraska climate and is able to thrive in areas with high heat and little water.

10. Wheat

Nebraska produces hard red winter wheat and hard white winter wheat, which are used in many types of breads and pastas. Wheat production in the state is valued at over $300 million each year.

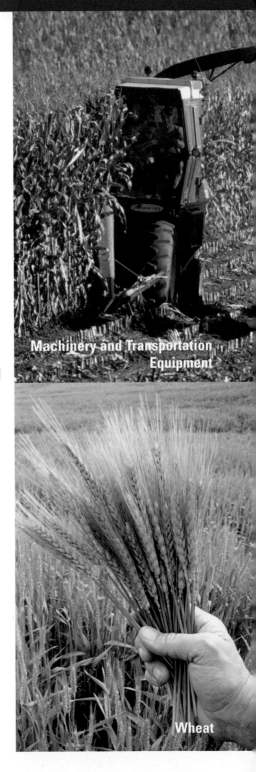

Machinery and Transportation Equipment

Wheat

Recipe for Potato Chip Cookies

Make any family get together a hit with this recipe for potato chip cookies.

What You Need

¾ cup (180 milliliters) butter

¾ cup (180 mL) white sugar

1 egg yolk

1½ cups (360 mL) all-purpose flour

¾ cup (180 mL) crushed potato chips

½ cup (120 mL) chopped walnuts

What To Do

- Have an adult help you preheat the oven to 350 degrees Fahrenheit (175 degrees Celcius).
- With the supervision of an adult, mix the butter and sugar together in a medium bowl until it's smooth. Then stir in the egg yolk, add the flour and nuts, and mix it all together.
- Next, stir in the potato chips so that they don't get too crunched up.
- With the help of an adult, roll the dough from the bowl into walnut-sized balls. Place the balls 2 inches (5 cm) apart from each other on a cookie sheet.
- Bake for ten to twelve minutes in the preheated oven. Lastly, have an adult help you remove the cookies from the sheet to cool on wire racks.

Indian Cave State Park is one of the many major tourist attractions in the Cornhusker State.

Scotts Bluff is another unexpected sight, rising out of the prairie. A huge plateau, it towers 800 feet (244 m) above the land. The peak can be reached on foot or by car and offers sweeping views of the countryside for more than 100 miles (161 km) in all directions. These two unique features became well known to the pioneers making their way across the plains along the Oregon Trail. Like prairie signposts, they marked the end of roughly one-third of the journey from Kansas City to the West Coast.

Also found in the Panhandle is one of the nation's richest fossil beds. Preserved so it can be studied and enjoyed by countless generations, Agate Fossil Beds National Monument allows visitors to peer deep into the ancient past. The park contains the fossil evidence of the wealth of mammals that lived in the region during the Miocene epoch, twenty million years ago. Clearly Nebraska was a much different place then. Small two-horned rhinoceroses, 10-foot- (3 m) long predator pigs, and another mammal—described as a combination of a horse, giraffe, tapir, and bear—roamed the grasslands.

Among the most unusual finds at the site are the preserved burrows of a land beaver called *Paleocastor*. Like today's prairie dogs, these large rodents lived together in dens tucked deep beneath the

Popcorn Producer

Nebraska produces more popcorn than any other state. Its yield was more than 270 million pounds (122 million kg) in 2013.

surface of the plains. They created spiral-shaped burrows that spun around and around deep in the ancient riverbanks. Early discoverers of the twisting chutes were baffled, calling them Daemonelix, or "devil's corkscrews." Scientists believe the unique structures may have been used to confuse and stop curious predators that entered the burrows in search of a meal.

People also come to Nebraska to watch the migration of the sandhill cranes. Two recent million-dollar projects have taken great strides in ensuring the safety and future of Nebraska's beloved seasonal visitors. The Crane Meadows Nature Center, located outside Wood River, offers three blinds—or enclosed shelters—to morning and evening visitors. To the west, the National Audubon Society's Lillian Annette Rowe Bird Sanctuary in Gibbon offers bird watchers four blinds. The famed nature magazine *National Geographic* has also set up a live, online video feed of the cranes for those who cannot make it to the site in person.

The birds have become popular tourist attractions, each year drawing more and more people from across Nebraska and around the world. With these two new centers, humans and cranes now have the ideal settings in which to coexist. Wildlife centers such as these show that Nebraskans wish to provide a safe, welcoming place for all its visitors, whether they be animal or human.

Manufacturing, Services, and Retail

Nebraskans make and manufacture a variety of items. Clocks, magnets, furniture, fans, golf clubs, and pipe organs are just some of the things produced in the state. Workers also produce large-scale items in some of the state's major factories. The creation of machinery, farm equipment, and car parts helps keep people employed. The state usually has an unemployment rate well below the national average. In August 2015, the rate in the state was 2.8 percent, compared to the nation's 5.2 percent. The state's farmers need to be able to plant and harvest their crops. Truck drivers, too, must be able to transport farm products to processing centers across the state. It is not surprising, then, that a successful industry has emerged in the state by supplying workers with these items.

Since Nebraska is such a major agricultural state, food processing is also big business. Currently the processing and creation of food products is the state's largest source of income. Dairy items, meats, and flour and flour-based products such as cereals and pasta are just some of the foods that are prepared in the Cornhusker State. Workers also process grain to feed to the state's large herds of livestock.

Researchers in a lab in Omaha study ways to improve the growth of trees and crops in Nebraska.

These various business operations can be found across the state. The state's largest economic center, though, is Omaha. Slowly through the years, the city has emerged as a major business center. Food processing, insurance, telecommunications, and health care are just some of the major industries that keep residents of Omaha busy.

Lincoln is another business center. In addition to the University of Nebraska, which employs thousands of people, the state capital hosts a wealth of companies that produce medicine and related medical products, transportation parts and equipment, and many other things. Insurance and telecommunications are important Lincoln industries as well.

It takes a wide range of Nebraskans to keep the state productive and strong. Doctors, mechanics, cooks, librarians, and real estate agents are just some of the many roles state residents fill in order to serve and assist their fellow Nebraskans. To many of the state's citizens, the pioneer spirit is still alive, and helping each other out is not an old-fashioned notion. Though the state has changed a lot since the days Native Americans roamed the plains, Nebraskans know that whatever challenges the future brings, they will face them together.

NEBRASKA
STATE MAP

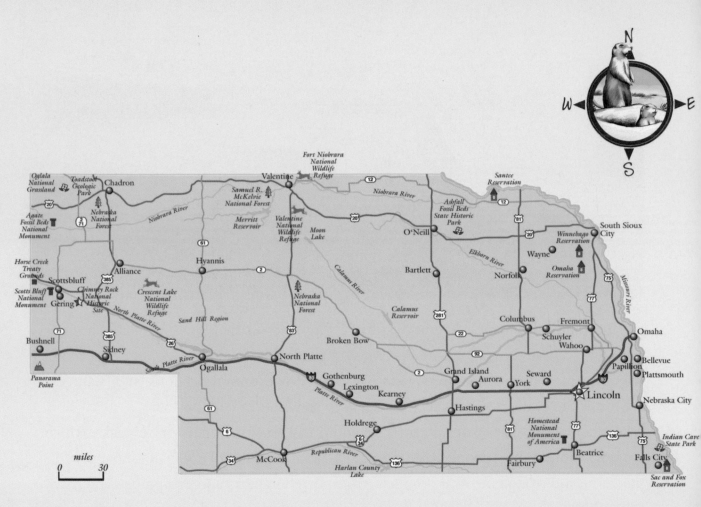

N
W   E
S

Oglala National Grassland
Toadstool Geologic Park
Chadron
Samuel R. McKelvie National Forest
Valentine
Fort Niobrara National Wildlife Refuge
Santee Reservation
Niobrara River
20
Agate Fossil Beds National Monument
Nebraska National Forest
Niobrara River
Merritt Reservoir
Valentine National Wildlife Refuge
Moon Lake
20
O'Neill
Ashfall Fossil Beds State Historic Park
81
12
South Sioux City
71
61
Hyannis
2
Calamus River
Bartlett
Elkhorn River
Wayne
Winnebago Reservation
Horse Creek Treaty Grounds
Alliance
385
Crescent Lake National Wildlife Refuge
Nebraska National Forest
Norfolk
Omaha Reservation
Scottsbluff
Chimney Rock National Historic Site
Sand Hill Region
83
Calamus Reservoir
281
Columbus
77
Missouri River
Scotts Bluff National Monument
Gering
North Platte River
Broken Bow
22
Schuyler
Fremont
75
Bushnell
71
385
Sidney
Ogallala
North Platte
2
Grand Island
92
Wahoo
Omaha
Panorama Point
South Platte River
26
Gothenburg
Lexington
Kearney
Platte River
Aurora
York
Seward
80
Papillion
Bellevue
Plattsmouth
61
6
Holdrege
Hastings
81
Homestead National Monument of America
77
Lincoln
136
Nebraska City
Indian Cave State Park
34
McCook
Republican River
61 34
136
Fairbury
Beatrice
75
Falls City
Harlan County Lake
Sac and Fox Reservation

miles
0   30

— 🐃	Interstate Highway	•	City or Town	🗻	Highest Point in the State	
— 🛡	U.S. Highway	🌲	National Forest	🏛	Indian Reservation	
— ⬭	State Highway	🗼	National Monument	🦫	State Park	
★	State Capital	🦌	Wildlife Refuge	★	Historic Site	

NEBRASKA
MAP SKILLS

1. What is the highest point in the state?

2. What is the state's capital?

3. How many national forests are there in the state?

4. If you were driving from Lincoln to Grand Island, which direction would you be traveling?

5. Which pair of cities are closer to each other: Columbus and York, or Fairbury and Wayne?

6. Which national forest is closest to Valentine?

7. Which city is farther from Indian Cave State Park: Nebraska City or O'Neill?

8. Which two major roads meet near the Santee Reservation?

9. Which city is not along Route 2: Broken Bow, Lincoln, or Hyannis?

10. What's the closest city to South Sioux City?

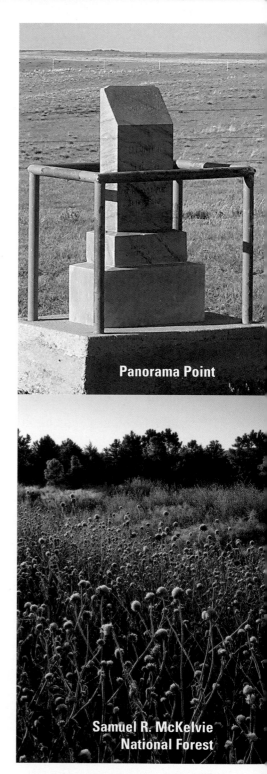

Panorama Point

Samuel R. McKelvie National Forest

10. Wayne
9. Lincoln
8. Routes 81 and 12
7. O'Neill
6. Samuel R. McKelvie National Forest
5. Columbus and York
4. West
3. Three
2. Lincoln
1. Panorama Point

State Flag, Seal, and Song

Nebraska was one of the last states to adopt its own official flag. In 1925, lawmakers set out to design one, adopting a banner that consisted of "a reproduction of the Great Seal of the State charged on the center in gold and silver on a field of national blue." Although it was technically adopted in that year, at the time this important symbol was called the "state banner." It was not named Nebraska's official flag until 1965.

In 1867, one of the bills lawmakers adopted called for the creation of the state seal. It would show "a steamboat ascending the Missouri River; the mechanic arts … represented by a smith with a hammer and anvil; in the foreground, agriculture to be represented by a settler's cabin, sheaves of wheat, and stalks of growing corn; in the background a train of cars heading towards the Rocky Mountains, and on the extreme west, the Rocky Mountains to be plainly in view; [and] around the top of [the] circle, to be in capital letters, the motto: 'Equality Before the Law.'" Finally, circling the seal are the words "Great Seal of the State of Nebraska, March 1st, 1867."

The state song is "Beautiful Nebraska." Jim Fras wrote the music in 1960, and Fras and Guy Gage Miller wrote the lyrics. The composition was made Nebraska's official state song in 1967. Lyrics to "Beautiful Nebraska" can be found at: **www.50states.com/songs/nebraska.htm#.VjKtaRCrQyk.**

Glossary

agriculture	The production and raising of crops and livestock.
border	The boundary line that separates one country, state, or county from another.
civil rights	Rights to personal liberty that were established for African Americans as part of the Thirteenth and Fourteenth Amendments to the US Constitution.
climate	The weather conditions in a particular area over a long period. These conditions can include temperature, air pressure and quality, precipitation, and more.
conservation	The official supervision of natural resources in order to preserve them.
crop	A plant grown for food. These can include plants that produce grains, fruits, and vegetables.
drought	An extended period of time when there's little or no rainfall.
explorer	A person who investigates or travels through unknown regions.
frontier	The limit of settled land, beyond which is wilderness.
irrigation	The application of water to assist in the production of crops.
loess	A yellow-brown loamy (type of soil) deposit that was blown by the wind and built up in the Midwest.
mineral	A substance that occurs in nature, usually of crystal structure.
pioneer	A person who is among the first to explore or settle a new country or area.
reservation	A piece of public land that is set apart for Native American tribes.
slavery	The practice of owning another person who is forced to do what you want them to do.
tourism	The promotion of travel for vacations or to see places of interest.

More About Nebraska

BOOKS

Monnig, Alex. *Nebraska Cornhuskers*. Inside College Football. Edina, MN: ABDO Publishing, 2013.

Plain, Nancy. *Light on the Prairie: Solomon D. Butcher, Photographer of Nebraska's Pioneer Days*. Lincoln, NE: Bison Books, 2013.

Weatherly, Myra. *Nebraska*. From Sea to Shining Sea. Danbury, CT: Children's Press, 2009.

WEBSITES

Nebraska for Kids
www.visitnebraska.com/kids

Nebraska State Historical Society–Kids! Stuff
www.nebraskahistory.org/oversite/kidstuff

Nebraska Wildlife Federation
www.nebraskawildlife.org

ABOUT THE AUTHORS

Pete Schauer is a digital marketing manager, content producer, and freelance writer who lives in New Jersey.

Doug Sanders lives in New York but spent one of his favorite vacations exploring the Nebraska Panhandle. Highlights of the trip were stops at Toadstool Geologic Park, Fort Robinson, and Agate Fossil Beds National Monument.

Index

Page numbers in **boldface** are illustrations. Entries in **boldface** are glossary terms.

Index